A Butterfly Effect

ISBN#: 978-1-257-91218-6

I have 365 reasons to throw away 19 memories

And I have 12 reasons to cry 52 tears

And for the last 24 hours I've been trying to tell
myself that I still have 1 chance left

-Philip Dean 12/27/2010

I dedicate this book to Halie.

"May I one day forgive you for what you have done to me"

The following albums of poetry mark the consequences through which I have suffered all for the sake of love. May I never be that stupid again.

Two Months Of Solitude

<u>A Momentary Lapse of Treason</u>

A Chapter Between The Books

A past clouded over from dawn to dusk

A memory washed over doomed to rust

It's been a long time ago

But it seems so short

There's a new chapter to unfold

But the pages lie still in my silence painted court

This is my life I leave behind

It's all I've ever known

If only my clock would rewind

I'd make some changes of my own

But it ends now

Like an abrupt shattering of glass

And if justice remains to be found

I'll bury it in my past

For the wrongs I've done, I have no reason

It was all a momentary lapse of treason

Torture Of The Redeemed

I used to be afraid of the dark

I used to be afraid to hold my heart

Now I am mute despite my screams

Now I am a crashing wave falling upon idle dreams

A reverberating theme throughout my life

A reverberating rip and slash and tear and scream with a soft spoken knife

Set apart this Knightmare of mine

Set apart this torture of mind

Agonizing beauty that tells of safety

Agonizing pain of loss that seems to hate me

Ripped apart his soul to save her

Ripped apart his life to blame her

A love so deep that sickness bleeds

A love so deep with devilish deeds

A spoken word so soft that tears fall freely

A spoken word so hard so she won't see me

Crying pain that envelopes empty space

Crying pain that leaves no trace

I used to be afraid of the dark

Now I'm left with half of my heart

No Longer Is He

SOMEONE once asked me why I try

And I told them I didn't exactly know why

Maybe it was just a moralistic conception of my mind

Or maybe I was this simplistic one of a kind

PLEASE tell me what compels you to help others despite your own well-being

The stranger asked me with complete sincerity while completely forgetting with whom he was speaking

With a sigh I told him he had asked the wrong person the right question

He coughed and rubbed his forehead with an obvious sign of perplexion

SAVE me the trouble next time when I ask you about the important things of the world I knew

I had simply heard that if anyone around here would help the world it would be you

But now I realize you have finally been beaten and care not about the world and those lost

But one more question sir, your soul? For your soul, what was the final cost?

ME and my affairs are completely my own I answered

But if you must know, I once was unprotective of my soul so securely mastered

Tethered to my very beating heart it was in a time long adjusted

But it was ripped out and torn to pieces by someone I should have never trusted

FROM that day forward I was never the same

And on her head I place all the blame

If I could, I would erase every moment I ever spent with her

So that it could miraculously save me and keep me in a place I deemed much better

THIS, alas, is not the case and today you stare at a man who is beaten and bruised
Someone whose soul was despicably abused
If you would have asked me this question a year before
I would have been able to convey an answer far better and of much glorious grandeur

IMPENATRABLE days have flown by since then
And now I tell you once again
The reason that I tried is not answerable
Because as it seems, all hearts are not entirely impenetrable

DARKNESS comes to all those who believe they can make a difference
I thought I could and the world repaid me with a terrible offense
So now you come before me, an old veteran of a war never won
And I'd tell you more but, alas, I must depart with the rising of the sun

What I Was

I was a mountain

Standing tall amongst the watery atmosphere

I was a fountain

Flowing low between the crevices of your deafened ear

I was an eagle

Soaring high amongst the birds of prey

I was a seagull

Picking at the crumbs of a society wasting away

I was a tree of cedar

Rising high amongst the canopy below

I was a lowly creature

Buried beneath a mantle of snow

I was a leader

Falsely risen above the rest

I was a preacher

Screaming for his iniquities to be put to the test

I was a warrior

Corrupted by pride and power

I was a courier

Bringing messages of my collapsing tower

Now I'm a shadow

A trace of what I once was

Now my breathing draws shallow

A glimpse of my death before my life's pause

I once knew a girl

Whom I tricked myself into loving

She ruined my world

And now my life fades to nothing

Simply. Existing.

How do you rewrite a life long lived

How do you erase all the memories you wished you'd never dreamed

How do you go back to all the longing days

When in your heart, there is no going back

When in your heart, you can't undo the things you've said, done or seen

You can't unknow some of the people you've acknowledged

You can't forget something that is stenciled upon the cerebral fluids enveloping your brain

I feel like too little butter, spread across a plain of too much bread

I'm spread out, weak, insufficient

I'm only a shadow of the things that I once was, what I once dreamed

A mere spectral trace of a day that seems to be only yesterday

A day that's years apart but seems only hours ago

A day that was so calculated, so examined

Whatever happened to the day where I didn't care about the opinions of others

Whatever happened to the day where I was actually happy

ACTUALLY HAPPY, not the facade we put on to fool others and ourselves

As if I could convince myself that I was simply happy

If I could take back every moment, every second I spent in those seven long months I would

But that day was yesterday, and I live in a life I call today

Not tomorrow, not then, or in a day to come, but today

And I hate today, I loathe today

Because compared to my speculation of the past, today simply does not cut it

I simply exist

And this existence is the bare minimum

I simply exist in a world longing for the past

Longing to travel back to the past and rewrite history

As if history could be full of surprises

Today I live a life alone, empty, standing naked in the dark

No hope, no goals or ambitions, simply existing

Living vicariously through the past

And now I leave this untrained thought, this unfinished thought, this ambiguous thought

Empty and alone, like a strain of pollen, drifting effortlessly against the willowed wind

Simply. Existing.

The Memories We Retain

I was the rock that stood against the storm

I was the seam that remained together against that which was torn

But in all these things, only one thing still remains

A spectral trace of the evil done of long past days

And now there is a solitude amongst the past

A safety I wish that would always last

A time where I lived carefree and content

If only I knew the preciousness of the moments I had spent

If I could throw away some of the moments I would

And I would have done the things I knew I should

But sadly throughout the ordeal of losing one's past life

The thing that seems to always remain is the icy cold memory of all the strife

When I gaze back at all the misery and all the hurt I stimulated

It seems so significant to any good or help I might have traded

Traded for good or for bad it's all meaningless now

There's no going back and I don't know how

How I'll ever make up for the things I've done

No longer am I the favored son

No longer am I the bright shining star

Now I am a wayward soul, like a dear trapped in the headlights of your car

I am crushed and ruined like the paper you toss away

That rolls through the wind that I breathed in yesterday

I am a blade of grass cut in the morning

That is gone in an instant without warning

This is goodbye to the world I once loved

To those who will remember I will be watching from above

My Retributive Return

I've got this heart beat pounding like a fiery drum in my head
I'm about to rupture out of this confinement like a shotgun pumped with lead
I'm gonna come back and if y'all think you can stop me you better sit back down
Because I'm gonna come back with a new vengeance this time around
For three long months I've stayed in seclusion
Brewing slowly to rise and come back with a swift retribution
I'm gonna rise like a phoenix of old, and rain down fire on your heads
Because while I sat locked away, y'all slept peacefully in your beds
I'm leaving behind all of those who claimed to be my friend
Because of your inaction, our relationship has finally come to its inevitable end
And for all of my enemies out there, get ready to lose what you never gained
Because with one fell swoop, I'll end everything that your evil has stained
I'm gonna rain down my fury upon the heads of all of those who let me burn
Like a volcanic eruption I'll spread these redemptive flames of hurt
Because when I do return, y'all better hang your heads in shame
Because none of you stood up to stop them from slandering my name

Dream At Your Own Risk

As I lie my head down to sleep
And to the never-ending drifts of time do I creep
I begin to wonder of the containment of dreams
The very things that tug at my imagination's seams

As I descend into an effortless slumber
And the characters that hover hazardously start to mutter
The sweet secrets of a world that doesn't exist
Despite reality's walls, the voices that whisper silent screams persist

And now I wish I could escape to a place that defies authenticity
Leave a place I've always known to hurt my credibility
I'd collapse away into a dreamful state and never come back
It's this fearful addiction that continues to attract

But as in every dream, they eventually conclude
And the tales that are pieced together become unglued
My happy world, my peaceful world, begins to collapse
And as I wake back up my happiness begins to relapse

If only their existence could exchange places
And all the evil people are replaced with happier faces
Like a dream, the memory of my world would fade away

And my dreams would finally be here to stay

However, despite the parallels that are drawn between either world
An emptiness invades as the corners of my consciousness is unfurled
My dreams are crushed and all hope is gone
Because I denied all reason and brought her along

My innocence depleted, my ambitions erased
They're swept away, gone, without a trace
How could I let so much evil pervade my dreams
How could I let this virus contaminate my brilliant imaginings

And now I sit here with my visions collapsed
Thinking fondly of a time that remains buried in the past
And now I warn the reader, I want them to know this
When it comes to life, dream at your own risk

Forgive Me Father For I Have Sinned

Forgive me Father for I have sinned
An imperfection that tries to blend
A hateful lust affair I wish would end
Forgive me Father for I am wrong
An addiction that's strung me along
I want to quit but it's just too strong
Forgive me Father for I am hurt
It's to this self-afflicted pain to which I constantly revert
It's with this addiction I constantly flirt
Forgive me Father I want to be healed
Come by night with Your mercy revealed
To Your will I want to humbly yield
Forgive me Father for I have sinned
A life full of which I want to repent
Lord come by morning and give me my second wind.
Forgive me Father for I have sinned

This Strength Within

I'm sitting with the lights off
Waiting for my rain to storm
I silently whisper so soft
Waiting for my hail to pour

I'm paralyzed by a knock on the door
I look over perilously as the static of my TV fills the room
Someone has ventured through this oncoming storm
A stark scent fills the air like a deadly perfume

This rain starts to pour warily upon the roof of my home
I slowly turn the knob to the door of my humble abode
I pull forward and listen to the wooden fixtures of my house torturously groan
I wonder what kind of adventurer travels down such a dark and weary road

What man would bare the troubles of this world to visit me on this night
Who could have gone through this hell just to see me
What man could stand up to such troubles of perilous plight
Who could compel such a man to come to be

There's thunder and there's lightning
There's a storm I can't subdue
And I listen to these things so frightening

And the clouds rolled black and blue

I wish I knew I had the strength to travel such a road of peril
I stop myself for a second as the weather seems to be a bit clearer
I open the door as if I were approaching some sort of herald
And I stare at myself staring back at me from a solitary mirror

Amongst My Ashen Remains Part 1

I walk around this empty apartment with thoughts running like children in my head
Their translucent ideology plays a mockery of me upon my bare-surfaced bed
A spark, a memory of a time long ago
When I didn't hate myself after I had spoke
A gentle step as the floorboards creak
I hear the silent evils whispering on my tongue when I speak
The white walls of my apartment look blandly back at me
As if they had nothing to do with the situation I happened to see
A rattling sounds behind me as I search my home for something new
A toasted slice of bread stares warily amidst my toaster slightly askew
Slightly awkward, slightly out of place
Sitting atop my refrigerator because there was no other space
It didn't fit in on the kitchen counter
Nor did it fit alongside the salt and pepper
So alas, it goes where no others join its solitary company
Where silence and remorse come a plenty
I ignore the newly toasted bread and walk outside to feel the cool summer's breeze
But it's only an icy chill that shivers my spine as if to only tease
A winter long awaiting and a summer long debating
To remove its stifling grip from a world still chasing
A freedom that never existed, never begun
These are the things my imagination has cruelly spun
A world where the good guys finish last and the evil never dies

Where the good boys run away fast and the good girls cry

Where the innocent are punished and the corrupt walk free

And I can't help that this is partly my fault that I have let it be

I hate them for doing this but I spurned their hatred

I deserve the malice, the death brought upon my blood sprayed red

My lights flicker out as my imagination winds down

And I look to be buried amongst this accursed ground

My red painted door closes behind me and the wind ceases to exist

But the screams that reverberate amongst the inside of my temples still persists

And I apologize to all those I've hurt and all those I've manipulated

I understand if the memory of myself is forever hated

For I, myself hate me just like you

But I still remain, still wondering what to do

Do I run or do I hide

Do I stay or do I try

Bring my hurt, my pain to surface the light

Ask for peace from those who would prefer a fight

Nay, I will remain out of sight

Amongst My Ashen Remains Part 2

I long to resurface, bring my face to light
Bring my heart to judgement solely contrite
I long to return to a world renewed
Forgotten of my existence except by you
Half of me desires to reign down destruction like I did once before
The other screams for repentance from a multitude or more
My dreams are plagued nightly by the thought of her family
Seeking retribution amongst my waking ephemeral tragedy
I've gone from housed to homeless
Spending four long nights in a dark parking lot amongst my own lowliness
I survive by coincidence but I make no attempt to start anew
These brutal scars are a painful reminder of a distant memory of you
My world submersed in misery, I crawl out of the darkness
A sorrowful feeling for myself and I recollect how I started this
I wish I could come back as if nothing happened
But my hopes of returning have swiftly blackened
If I go back, would I be ridiculed or turned away
If I go back, would I have the supplemental words to say
Alas, I can't take the risk of causing more harm
So I'll keep my eye on them from a distance not too far
They'll never see me, they'll pass below
I long to be back with them more than they know
This wasn't my choice, this wasn't my doing

Now I am walled out to sit in my wasteland slowly brooding

I never said goodbye to any of you that I held most dear

Perhaps we'll meet again in another year

I wish I could come back, I wish I could go

But I don't think I would be welcomed back home

So I walk into my memory studded house

With my misery; my disoriented, estranged spouse

So I sit here now, in an apartment so hollow

With a crowd of rioters willing to follow

I hush them as I imagine a church of peace

Where I was once great, but now am considered the least

Will they take me back, I doubt it now

If I can change things, I want to know how

So I lie here in silence, waiting for death

To sneak upon me with my last imagined breath

Aftermath

Bridges Don't Burn Unless They're Made Of Wood

It seems like a weight has dropped off my cold shoulder
As the embers from a life long ago gently smolders
I sit here waiting for something to change
While everything still feels exactly the same
I have to end this, I have to tie up loose ends
I have to forgive enemies I used to call friends
So I write out these words upon a white washed page
While my bell tolls a new dawn, a new age
I'm walking down a narrow cobbled street
Dark puddles of ambiguous fluids settle amongst my feet
Like a shadowy depth that stares blankly up at the sky
And to glimpse a smile out of the corner of my twinkling eye
I see why things have been this way
It refines me, makes me better for a harsher, colder day
The warmth of the sun offsets the bitter chill of this cold hour
When things get too cold, I'll run back to the One who is my strong tower

A Hastily Drawn Out Note

I spent so many days trying to avoid her, trying to stay invisible
So many hours where the simple doesn't seem so simple
I'm terrified to risk my face rising from the murky waters
But there's this carnal instinct shared between His son and my Father
I must seek reconciliation from a list of names
And hers sits at the top, staring down at me in shame
My flesh begins to burn away as it gives in to the Spirit
A gentle voice calms and soothes as He continues to whisper
Sweet words of confidence into His created ear
A peaceful shower of love spreads as I feel His presence draw near
My footsteps sound a symphony orchestra of their own
As I saunter over to a place I no longer call home
She's standing there, dumbfounded and surprised
Utterly astonished by the look in my eyes
I had an entire speech prepared
Something to end this bitter hatred her mother shares
A call for forgiveness and a sacrifice of pride
A hastily written note composed for my fear to hide
And she stands there and all she can say is "I'm Sorry"
...
...
...
So am I

Seven Months Spent On Ignorance And Immaturity

I gave you every amount of my wasting energy

And now I'm left with this chasing memory

I gave my all to you so that you could be at rest

I gave you exactly what you ripped right out of my chest

And when it came time for me to let you go

You became my most hated foe

I did everything for you so that you might relax

And you cut my future away with your legalistic axe

You ripped away that which was precious to me

And you've brought about this hatred that makes my wrists bleed

I tried to make you happy, and I obviously failed

But at least I tried where no other had prevailed

Now you've beaten me to the ground like a helpless slave

You're trying to put me behind iron bars as if I were a criminal of the present day

You face no punishment while I am soaked in torment and lament

And you sit aloft staring down at me as your mother demands another payment

Sucking the very life-force out of me and dooming me to hell

You must think yourself lucky that I have been silenced from my story to ever tell

I did everything for you so when I ended things you wouldn't hate me

But you delivered this sentence upon me in your spiteful effort to repay me

A Pocket Full of Empty Promises

I have a world I wish to escape
But I'm stuck here in a world I've always known
I have a cage that I unknowingly create
A solitary prison all to my own

An ageless perfume infiltrates my nostrils like a furious haze
I choke on the embers of this city I've loved
A timeless argument rings through my ears bringing back tears from previous days
As if there were some message I hadn't received from above

An abstract stroke of luck evades my walk
And a silver-tongued knife splits my very stride
Bringing deceit upon those with which I'd wish to talk
But everyone knows that all that's spoken is lies

I have squandered my existence
For a pocket full of empty promises
I have squandered my inheritance
For a father who is ashamed of a son of his

Now I lay here wondering what my future may hold
Will I stay here in a town where I have become my own ghost?
Or will I leave, leaving statues erected of myself inlaid, with gold?

While I ponder this, I drink away my hateful hosts

I say goodbye to a blue stained letter from the past
I say hello to a red stained cross that wishes to save my life
I scream over and over again to a past that went by so fast
I whisper silent secrets to a future empty of solemn strife

A Separate World of Numbness

I live in a world full of smog and vapor

I live in a world void of pen and paper

I have an idea of tranquility that never exists

I have a nightmare of chaos that continually persists

I love a numbness that envelopes my mind

I love an awareness that escapes my closing eye

I know this peacefulness that is empty of authenticity

I know this brutality that screams an unreal specificity

I hate this falsified feeling of happiness

I hate this testified feeling of loneliness

I am aware of a surreal mentality that fights within myself

I am aware of a normality that changes with amounts of superficial wealth

I am under an influence like a love-hate relationship

I am above a reassurance like a hypocrite of narrow accomplishment

I want to live a life I lived to the fullest

I want a life where I don't live it missing bullets

I live a life where the days mix together

I live a life I'll forget forever

Has It Always Been This Sad

I'm sitting here drenched in my own failure and sorrow
And I go about things as if it could all be turned around tomorrow
Now I sit here crying my eyes out over what I've lost
My moralistic soul has been ripped apart at such a small cost
A trusting heart that remains, still, hesitant
This smile is just camouflage against a world so expectant
Expecting me to fall, expecting me to crumble
Because I was a selfish, prideful, never humble
I've got those who would tear me down inches away
And the rest that would offer their help, are busy today

I feel like burning alive
I feel like doing something stupid
I feel like I want to run and hide
I feel like becoming a fugitive

I feel like I'm feeling low
I feel like I'm feeling high
I feel like I've lost my soul
I feel like I'm about to die

I wish I could go back to that day
I wish things never happened this way

Now I've got a body full of scars

Insignificant in quantity when you compare them to the stars

I would like to tear down these walls like a paper-thin defense

I would love to pass through these trials in one glorious attempt

But I'm stuck here, with walls at heights of which I can't begin to explain

So I'm stuck here, no hope, no plans, no love, no reason to complain

But I'm a liar, I'm a cheat, I'm an adulterer, I'm a sinner

The light of my faith grows impetuously thinner

And tonight, I wish You would save me.

Save me from myself.

Back Into This Hole

Once again, I'm sitting here.

Not moving, not doing anything.

Just sitting here hoping I can find someone with a listening ear.

A compassionate ear, a merciful ear, a wise voice,

Someone tell me something encouraging, something sweet,

Someone pull me up out of this rut I've begun to call home,

Someone save me, someone put me down to sleep,

Someone put me out of my misery.

What have I done to myself?

What have I done!

Where can I find someone willing to help?

What terrible acts have I committed?

I have turned my back on all I've ever known!

I have taken my eyes off something I believed in!

And now I'm dirty, lost and all alone...

And now I just want to go to sleep.....

I want to shut out all the dark memories..

I want to shut out all the sadness..

I want to shut out all the monstrosities!

I want to shut out these thoughts..

I have changed, and there's no going back.
I have shut myself off from the good in my life...
I have changed, and it's a terrible fact.
I have hidden myself from a shame, a guilt that knows all my hiding places,

No depth of mind, no matter how hard I try, it's always there.
This shame, this guilt I have beckoned to my doorstep!
And I run and I hide but there's never any room to spare!
I am trapped within my own shadowed thoughts...

I wish I could carve out my own little niche in my head..
So I could stay there forever, not feeling the outside world,
I wish I could cleanse away these feelings I dread,
But I can't, I'm stuck here and I'm not getting anywhere...

My existence lies wasted upon a cobbled road...
My achievements are meaningless to me...
Nearly nineteen years, and I've got nothing to show...
And now I wait for an end that will never come...

A One Way Vacation

Sunny shores, luscious forests,

Birds singing in one chorus,

Peaceful valleys, terrible mountains,

Ancient cities and broken fountains

These are the places you would go,

But the places you would not stay,

These are the faces you would know,

But the faces you would not trade,

I need a one-way trip to a destination uncertain,

No luggage, no baggage, nothing to take,

I need a new start with the unraveling of a crimson curtain,

Nothing to give, nothing to take, a future of my own to make,

Blue skies, flattened plains,

There are some things that blood will not stain,

Cracked roads, rolling hills,

And my heart yearns forever still

The Collapse

Cry To The Moon

I cry out in the night like a wolf does to the moon
All these memories washing down my face like tears over you
A cry of sadness, sorrow, and sin
A high-pitched shriek of madness, murder, and the fall of men
I cry out over the girl who brought my fall
And at my heart, I begin to rip, and tear, and claw
Trying to destroy the source of my pain, the source of my insanity
Trying to find a way through the destruction, through the calamity
And my cries echo plainly through the still of the night
Bringing back the sad tale of a heart contrite
Now it hurts in the worst way ever since I've fallen
Crushed bones, and crushed heart and my voice still cries to the moon, still calling
The moon looks down at me, unwavering, never caring
And the trees are the same, with the blank faces they are wearing
Not an animal stops to hear the message that is brought
Nothing cares; nothing notices a single tear that I've dropped

It Gets Worse

I hurt myself today

To see if it changed anything

But it didn't, and I still feel the same

I lost myself today

To see if I could come back

But I didn't, and I still feel the same

I longed to go back another day

To leave the pain behind

But I'm stuck here, with no other way

I wanted to visit yesterday

To change what I have heard

But I'm stuck here today

I tried to kill myself today

To end what I've become

But I failed again, a disappointment in a different way

I tried to end it this day

So I could forget the hurt

But I failed, and now I've got nothing else to say.

Leave Me Before I Hurt You Too

Just sink away into nonexistence

Just fall apart to your hateful forces

Just walk away with my teeth clenched

Just burn away like little torches

And now I sacrifice myself alone

It was an ultimate price

You're better off to never know

The memory of my life

And rip me from your caring arms

These tears you shed do no good

Leave before I cause you harm

So that you remember me as you should

But there's no use as I crumble now

Into the ruin of forgotten saints

Why it came to this, I wish I didn't know how

For people like me there is a secret place

So run away while there's still time

Far enough to forget my name

Run away before you find

These evil rewards that I have claimed

Leave me before I break your bones
Desert me before I begin to scream
About the iniquities of my regretful woes
And the destruction of my life's dream

Rescue me with your abandonment
And never look back again
Evade me like a contaminant
Like the infection of my sin

I only wish that you weren't my friend
I claimed to be someone so sweet
But I only hurt you in the end
And now my damnation is complete

So break me against these stones
So you can't recognize me anymore
Rip me apart so no one will know
This memory you've begun to abhor

A Time For The End: Part I

I don't want your pity
I don't want your love
I don't want this city
I think I've had enough

I've had enough of the hurt and the pain
I've had enough of the whispers and secrets
I don't like how you flirt in my face
I don't like how I get the silent treatment

I don't like how I'm turned away
Even though she is still treated oh so well
I don't like how I have to hide my face in shame
I don't like how my life is another sad story to tell

And now I wish to close the pages of this tale
And now I wish to close the seal on my fate
No more options to choose, no more lies to trail
No more doors to open, no more names to hate

I wish to end it all and never look back again
Forget the names of my friends
Forget how their caring starts to end

Forget how they let me hurt

Forget how they let that woman win

A Time For The End: Part 2

Forget how her evil worked
Or how she wrecked my life
Forget how she made me hurt
Forget all my pain and strife

I know I am partly to blame
And for this, I hate myself
I know how my memory is put to shame
So I reach out but receive no help

For who would help a wretch like me?
Who would help someone so low?
It's easy, almost plain to see
I'm someone you don't need to know

Forget I was ever here
So I can't hurt you, too
Forget I was ever near
It's time to find someone new

Now I wish to end it all, and forgot those who I've known
I wish to end it all, to forget my fading days
And leave this place I called home

I wish to never see her face

But when I close my eyes
There she is again
When I begin to cry
I seem at a loss for friends

I feel horrible for the things I've done
And here she comes to attack me
Adding on to my woeful story spun
Letting my world collapse slowly

She brings darkness to my eyes
Vanquishing the light I used to know
She brings desperation to my lies
To vanquish the light of my friendly foes

I am a creation gone bad
An experiment of cruel intentions
So I leave this world so sad
To give up on all past pretensions

A Heart Full Of Hatred

I have filled my heart with hatred
Compressed so tight it has become a bleeding stone
So heavy with doubt that's stained red
It has no nature of its own

I would burn away every pure desire
Just to know that I am whole
I would rip through her heart with fire
I would tear out her very soul

My eyes glow with a fiery rage
Rage fueled by anger and by pain
I would cleanse her name from this very page
And watch her life wash away in my rain

My heart is manifested with darkness
A fire so hot it shines no light
I would envelope their world and stop this
Have her swallowed by the night

My heart is full of hatred
Carved out into a hole
My victim's body stained red

With the bitterness of my soul

I Hate The Life You Love

I want to snuff out this flame that burns low
And let the smoke become a subtle memory from years ago
I hate this life you wish to save
I hate this life of which you crave
Leave me, forget me, lose me
Before you see the monster that I see
Every time I glimpse in this icy river, my fatal reflection
It screams of the perfect imperfection
The very skin that hangs from my disgraced bones
Cries out to a watery grave to become its new home
This heart you care for, cares for nothing
Yet you stay beside me as if I were someone you should be trusting
Go! Leave me behind to the ephemeral history books
Don't look back; don't watch me take this life in this arctic brook
For I will drag you under the icy water with me and watch as you drown
So that I can join you as my skull comes crashing down
You promise to save me, but you know not of what you speak
For I am an abomination to the warmth of life's fire you intend to seek
Deliver me into my dark, watery abyss
Or unite to my face your first and final fatal kiss
I loathe the very air I seem to breathe
As if it refuses to suffocate me so that I can leave
I wish to leave you and everyone else behind

And leave no trace of love or hate for you to find

This is my subjective punishment of which I long for

Your mercy is unwanted; I don't want your grace anymore

If you truly love me, let me go

Into these dark waters that ebb and flow

That pull away at my dwindling spirit

As my darkest hour calls me; I swear I can hear it

My hate is a poison, of which love can make no antidote

I want none, I need none, for my carcass is like a stone; it will not float

I will not resurface for the world to find me again

And your love can't save me, I'm sorry old friend

So give up on me like everyone else has

So too, your love shall come to pass

As my memory fades away like the flower in the harsh winter

I am just another thorn in your side, a forgotten splinter

And as the blood inside my veins freezes over

My mind begins to shutdown; a thought that is surprisingly sober

My cold heart of stone, cries out in crimson tears

And lets loose a flood that vanquishes the innocent's fears

My heart crumbles inwardly and begins to cry out in glee

For those who watch; let my death be as it should be

And now this icy feeling finally numbs all pain

As you watch in horror as I finally drift away

When The Church Becomes A Building

You traded decency for aristocracy

You traded your principles for hypocrisy

You traded your members for politics

You traded me for a simple, quick fix

You said you sided with me, but only I faced the consequences

You say I'm welcome but your judgmental stares are like prison fences

You call out for restoration but I still feel your unforgiveness

You kept me at an arms distance so I couldn't see this

I can't see how you have let her go freely

And to my death you have condemned me

If you wanted me gone, why didn't you just say so

So much for the church I thought I used to know

Meaningless

"Meaningless! Meaningless!" says the Teacher. "Utterly meaningless! Everything is meaningless."
Ecclesiastes 1:2

There is no point to go on

There is no point in working hard

There is no point in achievements

No point in family, friends or foes

There is no point in laughter, life or love

There is no point in happiness or sorrow

Everyone we will ever know, ever see or ever love

Fades away like the clouds in the sky

Everything we know is meaningless

Without cause, without significance

No considerable being or event will change a thing

Time keeps going, and time keeps forgetting

Time keeps no record of rights or wrongs

Time keeps no record of accomplishments or failures

Time keeps no memory of friends or loved ones

Time keeps going

And there's nothing you or I can do to stop it

Why even try, when in the end, awaits our own destruction

I am my own worst enemy

And I will bring about the cause of my ruin

And just as every other soul that has ever come into existence

So, too, will I be forgotten

And so will you

So why even try to make a difference?

Why even try?

Why even try?

Why even live...

Vampire

You draw blood
From my lip
You draw blood
With your fist
You draw blood
From my wrist

I bleed out
All alone
I bleed out
Far from home
I bleed out
On my own

I've got tears
Making tracks
I've got tears
Facing facts
I've got tears
Coming back

I cry out
All my fears

I cry out

All my tears

I cry out

Through the years

I fade out

Into gray

I fade out

From the day

I fade out

Far away

Of Suicides And Hopeful Failures

Steel

He looks down and sees his reflection

He looks back and sees a life of imperfection

This tool stares back at him with solid apathy

He asks a question, “Is this all you had for me?”

His hands are shaking with fear of the future

His hands are aching with pain mixed with anger

He turns it towards himself for a second or two

Not sure if he knows what to do

The cold grip of it lying silently in his hands

Is just like a coldness he knows, that tries to expand

And just like that, the evil deed is done

And his life force pours over the side and starts to run

The four corners of his room meet with crimson satisfaction

They’re haunted forever by this ill-fated action

The knife drops and lands on the floor

And his final dying breath escapes out his door

His arms a bloody mess of terrible desire

His life a tear-filled mess like a soldier-for-hire

He spoke of it many days in advance

And he went through with it at the mercy of his hands

Swallow

An orange container stares warily up at him

A small voice of pleading hangs on wearily to its plastic white rim

A tear trickles down the side of his worried cheek

Tilting his chin down at trembling hands so weak

In one hand, is an old photograph

The other wishes it could reach back into the past

Regret that is not quite so impossible to swallow, floods through his mind

And a wish that won't come true, requests to rewind

He drops the picture and pushes down on the lid

He grips tighter and twists what any other would forbid

A bend of the elbow, and a curious tilt of dread

A swallow of pain both existent here and all in his head

Memories and ideas drip away like a leaky pipe

Another painless end to another painful night

Stories

The wind blows through his hair up here
And it brings the scent of a terrible year
He looks around in awe of his situation
He's all alone with no one to face him
Down below, the people look like ants on a hill
Up above, the clouds look like islands lying still
He can see for miles up here on this ledge
And he can hear their laughter ringing in his head
A single tear falls far below
And it lands secretly so no one will know
A headline story he wanted to become
A headline story coming with the rising of the sun
It's quiet now, and the wind has stopped blowing
It's silent now, and his fear starts showing
It was his only answer, his only choice it seemed
And as his weight teeters over the edge, he wants to scream
Thirty stories up leads to one story coming down
A sigh of release escapes before he hits the ground
Like a stone he fell, through waters of sadness
Dead weight he was and to dead weight he had this
Thirty stories of flight were his last stories to read
Thirty stories up they'll remember always, indeed

Threads

Threads intertwined as one single strand

Looped around by shaking hands

Bark scrapes against sturdy sides

And a drop of water runs down in gentle tides

Branch after branch passes below

This is a secret place where no one should go

Tied it off to a limb large enough to stand

And the threads unfold once more in one single strand

A quivering lip and a single thought of doubt

Makes a mind insane enough to go this route

A quick drop and a snap as it bounces with force

A tightening of the rope shuts out all remorse

Tied to a branch that is large enough to hold

A body swaying limply, a body gone cold

Poison

There's a feast that could be fit for a king

Or for the lowliest of beggars all the same

The bread, the wine, the melting butter pools around his feet

The condiments lying quietly off of the beat

And he reaches slowly for a cup ordained to his hand

And a stillness settles around a table meant for one as he planned

A quiet layer of salt settles around his glass as he sips

And a cold shiver of remorse sinks deeply into his lips

As he bites surreptitiously into a piece that seems too big to take

He seems to forget the weight of the food that left him in this state

And as the drink and the food begins to settle again

He looks down at a cup he's come to call friend

He takes time to notice how the meal went by so fast

As he gradually remembers this meal is his last

The Prince I Welcomed

Through The Cracks Of My Door

He came in the night like a whisper leaks through a closed door
And he invaded my ears with his silver tongue leaving me yearning for more
He spoiled me, my memory of who I was and who I am
He crept into my mind and changed me into an evil monster running from a lamb
He was the puppet master pulling the strings over me
And I obeyed willfully as I sunk lower and lower into my borrowed misery
I begged for an end, I screamed out into his realm for a stillness to come
But it never did, and my eyes forgot the sight of a rising Son
Wrinkles stretched thin by time formed across my pallid face
And I forgot His name, I forgot how You taste
His presence in my life was like that of the tiniest sliver of light peeping through the crack in the door
The door my prince crawled through, the very same door I left open for this tyrant's war
And I fell upon my own battlefield to rot and manifest myself into his power
And no rescue came for me, no shining knight in armor, no golden hour
I was trapped, hopeless, lost and confused
So I ran back to a master whose trust I had abused
But He wasn't there anymore
You see, my eyes had forgotten how to see Him...

The Face In The Knight

I saw your face in my Knightmares again

Staring at me with this wicked little grin

Your teeth filed down to sharp, black needles

Injecting your toxin, leaving my fingers feeling feeble

Your hands swaying limply at your sides left an ominous presence of emptiness

Your sweet poison lingered temptingly upon your frayed gloves killing me quick

But I come back again, time after time I come back, to beg for my punishment

To fall to my knees, asking, praying for a swift end, and to bring my torture of replenishment

Ripping me apart, clawing me back to health, to begin the pain again

Habitual degradation that knows no merciful end

My hands are ripped from my bleeding wrists

And the rest of my face is torn apart by her devilish fists

Wrenching my heart out of my scar-ridden chest of lies

And watching it pump vigorously outside of my body by my very own eyes

I drain my own blood upon this unbiased floor

Bringing about my own suffering so I could entertain her more

I hate you, more so than I even hate myself...

And that... that should scare you beyond end...

My Nineteenth Birthday

I held a gun to my head today
Thought it might make the pain all go away
I cried a thousand tears today
Because my lips knew not what to say
I cursed my life today
Hoping that maybe these memories would begin to fade
I sat in silent sadness today
Trying to convince myself this was the only way
I wrote a pathetic poem today
Knowing it wasn't a home for these thoughts to stay
I got closer than ever before today
Couldn't get the nerve to do it anyway
I held a gun to my head today
What a way to spend my nineteenth birthday

The Devil's Feast

You ensnared me like a rodent to a trap

Taunting me, coercing me to jump at the sound of your thunder clap

You deceived me with instant gratification and more

While you whispered to me secretly through the cracks in my door

I became a mindless servant to your meaningless will

Not doing everything, but not doing anything as my essence of time began to spill

You tricked me with pride and false hope

You gave me these hands of steel with which my life force I would choke

Stealing away my innocence, my future and my past

And to think this happened so slowly, I came tumbling fast

I don't even care anymore, who I belong to, I mean

I can't see straight enough to even hope to dream

We, The Light Bulbs

Just a light bulb

Small and insignificant

It looks just like all the other light bulbs out there

It sits blank, unlit, darkened amongst the dozens of others just like it

Until one day, it's chosen

One day, it's spun into a socket, a source of energy

And one day, it is given purpose

Shining out amongst the shadows that would seem to overwhelm it

But nevertheless, it still remains, the same light bulb it was before

Small and insignificant

It has only changed from a realm of uselessness

To a realm of usefulness

But it still has no uniqueness

There are hundreds more pouring out light

Some pouring out bigger and stronger strengths than it could imagine

Just a light bulb

Shining bright amongst a world of light and darkness

Then one day, it begins to flicker

Amongst the two separate realms of light and dark

It leans towards one side, one minute, and to the other, the next

Flickering so dangerously, so ambiguously it begins to fade

As time goes on, it leans closer and closer back to where it began

Lifeless and dark, no purpose, no use

And still it has no uniqueness

For there are a million other light bulbs out there flickering into darkness

For only a moment it shines once more

As if it were making some final act of defiance against an impervious enemy

And then, as if it had never shined to begin with, it goes out

Its potential, its primary design, gone and it will never come back

And now it goes back to join all the other light bulbs

All the other light bulbs that shrink, break, and fade into nothingness

Nothing special about it, nothing unique

For after all

It's only a light bulb

To Surround The Wind

Staring at a suicide note on a windy day
Staring at the barrel of a pistol, hoping the pain will go away
Watching as the hairs stand up on your back
And watching them turn to gray

You've put this off for far too long now
And it's time to take a bow
Say goodbye to this world
And never turn back around

This world has turned its back on you
To leave you praying silently in your pew
But your screaming is much too loud
To hear God tell you something new

So you throw your inhibitions to the wind at last
And take off the weights that made you collapse
Under the pressure of the plight of the world
And sink into a slumber that you had hoped would erase the past

Ice Upon My Land

These icy drops of rain fall upon my sodden land
And force the little rivers of blood from my hand
I only wish that I could understand
Why I rebuked the One who was the foundation of my plan
Why my crops are dead to become profit for another man
I have only enough room to expand
A deadly wish, a wonderful nightmare with my right hand
A doom that settles along the shadows that lie upon my land
And my productions turn against me under the logo of a different brand
My own worst enemy stares at me from a mirror that refuses to stand
But lies flat upon the ground, covered by my hourglass' sand
And this hate I bear is what has done me in like a capital reprimand
To those of you who glimpse at this, I doubt you will understand

Bleeding Out The Impurities

I woke up spitting out blood this morning
And I spilled out your crimson name into my sink
And your name in my blood stared warily up at me
Wondering what my opinion would stand to summit
Dripping surreptitiously from my undying lips
The letters of your most hated name lingers still
Floundering aimlessly around the edges of this basin
And I relive the memory of our war enticed by hopes of peace
A war fought with lies and stupidity
A war started by veiled messages, veiled notes
Speaking of a love that couldn't be found
Lying of a love that never should have existed
And proving a stupidity that continually persisted
I woke up spitting out blood this morning
Exercising your evil from my infected teeth
Teeth that held onto your manipulated lips
Teeth that tore into my flesh bringing fresh blood
I bleed you through my skin, through my every orifice
And I leave you dripping, spilling, soaking in the bottom of my sink
Where you belong

He Discovered Fire, He Discovered Tragedy

The spark grows wilder like hair drifting in the wind

And a flame bursts forth like a flower's bloom begins

Growing stronger growing brighter

Brightness brings darkness to hearts of materials lighter

Tongues of hot evil lick at my hands, lick at my mind

Started out warm now it's a painful burn of which sobbing sorrows reminds

Got a wildfire tearing away at my inside's life forces

Manifesting and manipulating my moves, my thoughts, my choices

There's a blaze ripping me away from myself so old

And a gentle picture with a smile so faded it grows cold

Left to embers and ashes like a useless memory that hurts

Self destructive tendencies of an inferno that I chose first

And now that the fire's gone, it's easy to look around and see everything

See everything the heat took away; see that I'm left with nothing

Nothing but ashes that are just painful reminders of what I've lost

Something I've traded in at an ultimate cost

And these crisped bars lean over at me looming higher

Condemning me, the inventor, the producer of this fire

I Welcomed This Invasion

The prince invades me upon his own terms
And my walls lie dormant with only haunted traces of subtle words
Traces of scrawling letters are left upon my bedroom walls
Soaked in blood and sweat and tears from which my pen's ink calls
My defenses are torn down and my hosts replaced by judgmental stares
No champion left to defend my honor, no one left who really cares
I am left to the crumbs and dark corners of my household
And steadily marching, this prince comes knocking bold
Offering things such as riches and peace with concealed secrets of poverty and war
And I succumb to my own desires, my pitiful desires, my woeful desires for more
My foundation crumbling with icy veins leeching away my essence
You would have thought the first time I would have learned my lesson

I Am Blinded From The Light

Once inside, he manifested himself to my own selfish whims

And he traded with me innocence for sins

My fortress is his barracks, and his crows circle my head above

And I stand, arms folded, upon my terrace, but he won't budge

My body, weak and feeble, my bones collapse

And as if on instinct, the crows react

Biting, tearing, ripping and shredding until I remain only through sad memory

I am left with nothing but pity and sorrow for me

My blood spilled upon the darkened ground

Stained by a poison I hoped I'd never found

First they wrench out my eyes so I cannot look above for light

Then they devour my hands, so I can't put up a fight

My shame reaches its highest multitude as I am feasted upon by these birds

And my potential spills out, empty of its crafty words

They hack through my laid back shoulders, my arms and my unmovable legs

They disembowel my stomach though my silent screams continue to beg

Begging for a swift end only I alone choose to bring

But my resolve still remains too weak

My lips are torn away and my tongue dissolved in the sky

My hair ripped out with the last remaining wisps of my desperate cry

And they slash and hack and burn through my heart

Choking on their beaks penetrating my lungs from a delayed start

And I lie mutilated on the soiled ground of hallowed lives

And the crows take underground, the last of my heaven seeking eyes

The Untitled

Prologue

Standing on the edge

The edge of a building, the edge of a sword, the edge of a cliff

Part One: Flashback

I've sunk so low the weight of the water crushes bone, heart, and mind

I've been in the dark for so long now I have become blind, deaf, and hopeless

And I nearly erased myself from existence

In fact I tried to

But once more... I failed

And once more I fell

Deeper, farther, faster, harder

There was no bottom deep enough for me

No torture painful enough for me

After my skin had been flayed from my wretched bones, these hateful bones

Part Two: Subtle Realization

A single drop of water fell to my depths

A single drop fell so that I could rise

Not to the surface, but close enough

Close enough that my blind eyes might open and see

A single ray of minuscule light

With scars littering my entire body, heart, and mind

I fought the light

I fought what I used to embrace

And once again I failed

Part Three: Path Of Its Own

So now I stand on the edge of this building, this sword, this cliff

And I look down into the depths I still call home

To see that I've found my resolve

My resolve to leave the home that brought me the pain I craved

So I've come to this cliff, this edge, this fork in the road

One leading back down the way I've known

One leading back up the way I came

And I hold animosity towards both paths

But only one fury is a rightful fury

And then I look at the road within myself

The path that takes no paths but makes them all of its own

And I hate that road, too if not more

Epilogue

So now where do I go?

Foretold Stories Of Redemption

Drip, Drip, Dripping

Water drips tediously along a leaking pipe

Sucking away at the pulsating veins of my life

Memories drip away eroded by apathetic hours

And forgetfulness replaces abhorred dreams in secret little showers

Drip, drip, dripping from a ceiling that knows no bounds

But it seems so constricting, cramped up with all these booming sounds

Yelling, screeching, screaming my name with murder dripping off their lips

They crucify me with their words, sucking my hope away with their betraying kiss

But I stare back with fire set in my eyes

I brush away their evil whispers, their pretty little lies

So I struggle back to the leak in my veins

And set the cracks right with a list full of names

Crossed out with blood and tears and tears and tears

And I set out once more, dripping away the injury of this painful year

Leaving the pools of tears mingled with blood

To waste away with the drip, drip, drippings of hated love

I've Ripped Out This Hate

If I turn you inside out, what will I see
Will I see the same monster that was inside of me
If I turned you around, what will I find
Will I find your dirty little secrets you tried to hide
If I flipped you upside down, what will I discover
Will I discover all the ugly shadows you've tried to cover
If I dove deep inside your skin, what will I meet
Will I meet the despicable demons I used to keep
If I sat you in front of a mirror, what will I perceive
Will I perceive all the lies with which you would try to deceive
If I ripped open your heart, what will I display
Will I display the same hate that I ripped out of my heart yesterday

The Thief Upon My Hill

The pitter patter of your toes tremble upon my icy ground
Quietly drifting towards my still body, making not a sound
The dead blades of grass break as your foot steps quietly in fear
And they fall softly to the ground like my solitary tear
A stained glass memory containing seven months of a heaven so false
Followed by seven months of hell that came at such a heavy cost
And your feet continue their pitter patter, pitter patter up my hill of lies
While your trail is followed like an assassin with a thousand eyes
Watching your pitter patter, pitter patter through my secret thoughts
Rummaging and scavenging for the secrets you've always sought
And I lie ever still upon the peak of my silent hill
Waiting for your discovery, for your prize to steal
It's not here anymore, I burned it along with your name
I've cast you back to the fiery pit from whence you first came
I've rebuked your presence amongst my hill of shadows for the last time
Once you realize it's not here anymore; then you'll know your crime
And so your pitter patter will become a fleet of foot as you escape my consciousness
And you realize I have risen up with nail-pierced hands above my adorned head of preciousness
Your pitter patter, pitter patter fades away into the darkness that once manifested my mind
For you've finally noticed there was no emptiness left here for your greedy hands to find

Ripping Off The Armor That Weighs You Down

It's fading now
Falling off my sweat drenched body in little bits
Falling down the curvature of my back, escaping into their hellish pits

His influence has escaped my fingertips' embrace
And I have begun to remember the comfort of Your face
You have separated me from the shadows I grew
So that I could draw near and be one with You
These curses roll off my shoulders like a world-weary stone
Curling up into little fists of fear, defending themselves all alone
The history lies dormant in its regretted past
And I have learned to outlive its hateful sneers at last
I shed this anger, depression, and stinging loneliness
Like a layer of my own skin, I can't believe I would resort to this
The scars of the past are fading now
And the healing begins, as my heart takes a lowly bow
Saying farewell to a world not loved nor forgotten
But left behind for its memory to become sodden
Soaked through with the tears of my hate
I have come to forget this of late

It's fading now
Leaving my bloodstream like poison from a wound

The only thing left to remind me is you

My Bleeding Lips

Staring north for a new revolution
And crying out for a safe revelation
Wiping tears away with scar marked wrists
A cruel reminder of the souls Satan twists
But I've found a place I can run to when I'm down
And I've found an ear I can scream to when I'm lost and never found
I was hidden away like a lost diamond in the sand
Forgetfulness and hatred being brought forth by the back of his hand
So I swallow pain like the very pill prescribed by death
Infecting my body, my soul, cutting off my last shallow breath
And it's all forgotten now, like a ephemeral shadow from the past
Crawling forth, out of my mind like the demon's whispers silencing me fast
And I've come too far to give up on this life
And I've fallen so hard to give up on the search for my wife
So I'm staring north for a new revelation
And forgetting their curses from an ancient revolution

Duo Of The Victors

The Falsity

There's just no way that we can live

When we've lost all that we could give

Lost all our possessions on a road of false hopes

Seen our friends hanging from your devil's ropes

And now we're slaves to their pity

Lost souls roaming the shadows of a lost city

And now we look forward to our apathetic ends

To fall to the depths of our forgotten friends

Down But Not Fallen

There's no time to pity the past

When our judgement approaches us fast

It's time to hold back no more

To unleash our retribution upon our enemy's door

We will bring redemption to our memories

And cast down the image of our faithless enemies

Bring up your chin love of mine

For the day we rise up once again has met its time

The Encounter

We are the remnant of those we once knew

And we come today to bring judgement upon you

We bring lightning that crashes across the sky

And with our philosophy of love, we make demons' hate die

Take hold of your last breath you foul beast

Before we hurl you back to the imprisonment of the least

We hold in our minds the power to execute you from the world we know

And slay you with our one last vicious blow

The Rebuttal

We call the remnant of the world to break loose your chains

And bring down your fire like a devastating rain

We will crucify you with the power of One

The time of your fateful defeat has finally come

We come to throw you back to the hell you've brought

And restore the inner mind that we've always sought

A synchronization that overwhelms your every move

We will stand fast, we will not lose

The Victors Of A Wasteland

Now we stand high atop your smoking carcass

Laughing at the idea you held to outsmart us

We hold high the achievements of victory

Securing our names upon the future minds of another history

We have smote you upon this infamous hill

And holding fast to our ever-pounding hearts of steal

You, our enemy, have fallen to your own demise

And we have risen to put a stop to all your lies

Upon this hill our enemy was felled

And now we are the kings of a nation you once held

And So It Ends At An Old Beginning

This old wagon wheel keeps turning slow

Steadily rolling over the rocks in its road

Steadily pushing away from a tumultuous past

And over these memorable rocks, this wheel will try to outlast

This wheel of wood and tears and blood passes far out of sight

Into a future that, at first, didn't seem so bright

And as the wheel's master seeks a retributive return

It rolls over a bridge that won't ever burn

But now that the load doesn't seem so heavy

The Wheel's master knows it might be ready

To face the promises and curses of a day not here

To forget the troubles of a past that seems so near

So this wagon wheel keeps rolling past the dead blades of grass

Passing a hill where my demons fled my dreams at last

Passing a wilted red rose that lies dormant upon the floor

Passing an opening, a crack through my puppeteer's door

Rolling past a mirror knocking at its owner's residence

And leaving behind the threads, the steel, the poison, the stories that swallowed the evidence

Crushing a dying light bulb as if it were insignificant or less

Rushing past the screams that still beg to confess

All the lies and the hate and manipulative thoughts that spoke

They are but ephemeral wisps upon the wind like a forgotten ghost

So this wheel, this wheel of wood keeps traveling on

Noticing all the rhymes it deemed forever gone

And this master behind this wheel remembers all these things with a stained glass tear

To wipe away a separate world of numbness from a bitter, sorrowful year

All the while, this wagon wheel keeps on turning to a future so bright

Leaving the question to the master, "Did you enjoy the ride?"

Extra Content

Abandoned

You abandoned me
To my own cruel devices
You abandoned me
To a world swallowing crisis

We used to be such great friends
Like that of which could never end
Now our time together sits as that of remnants of a past
A past I long for that never longs for me to relapse

You gave up on me because I consumed my life
And you left me behind before I could cause any more strife
You used to be there for me, as I was for you
But I drew selfish desires amongst my pitiful crew

My mind is a waste without your presence, your influence
I waste away without help or sanctitude from the worthless pursuit of meaningless affluence
My body contorted into wicked shapes and designs of pain
And my mind is changed to harness an evil that I thought I'd never gain

I hate you for leaving me to ruin and wreckage

I hate myself for letting you leave me to fix this
I am powerless to change by myself, alone
And I hate you because you knew I would destroy myself all on my own

Your inaction is just another cause to my end
I hate to say I still need you to be my friend
I am incapable of saving myself from my own desires
Like a forest, I will burn away from memory by the tongues of my vicarious fires

I only ask for help that helps anyone but me
If only this one chance could set me free
But I am wasted amongst the potential of design
And from your memory, I so quietly resign

You abandoned me
As I abandoned myself
You abandoned me
Still crying out for help

One Wilted Rose

He calls her for the last time today
She hears him say he's throwing his life away
Pleading erupts with an uncovered sob
Today is the day that another life is robbed
The phone drops suddenly from his ear
It lands on the floor but everything still sounds so clear
His crying sounds with love long lost
He was about to pay the ultimate cost
Screams erupt now from the speaker of his phone
A realization that he's finally all alone
A flash of steal and a click of the chamber
Tears fall freely but you can't really blame her
She meant everything to him but he lost it anyway
He could care less about his life this day
Shooting pain flows from her heart as she listens with deafened ears
She'd never forget this moment for many many years
A single bullet cartridge flies through the air
It's joined by small drops of blood when he had little to spare
It seems to fly forever; flipping noiselessly through space
The cartridge hits the wall and lands next to a vase
A wilted red rose lies deep inside
Droplets of red hit the vase and begin to slide
The wilted rose seems to feel his pain
Blood splatters against the walls like rain
On the other end she falls to the ground with a silent heave
She grips at her heart finding it hard to breathe
A petal falls from the rose and lands on the ground
It lands next to a body lying face down
Blood envelopes the petal and races for the corners of the room
The phone is sprinkled in blood from this preventable doom
Blood drips down the wall like paint on new paper
His soul evaporates into a tiny vapor
This wasn't how it was supposed to end
She felt the death of her greatest friend
She screamed his name for hours and hours
She saw the room and the wilted flower
The water in the vase a diluted red

The rose was lying there in the vase so dead
A petal lies on the floor next to his hand
He had gone out just the way he planned
She rushed to his side and picked up his face
The blood still dripped where the bullet flew through space
She thought about all the things she had done wrong
His eyes stared blankly but his gaze was held strong
Her lips came down to meet his for one last kiss
And if she forgets all the rest he wants her to remember this
This was his choice his loss his path
She was only a chapter in the story of his uneventful wrath
The blood trickled down and pooled at her knees
He wasn't there, but he was swaying through the trees
His soul had vacated that place and left her alone
Now it was her turn to make it on her own
She didn't want to live in a world where he did not exist
So she picked up the gun and followed him into the eternal abyss
There they lay two lovers on the ground
They lived together and died together but they emitted no sound
When they found them their hands were held as one
Her last breath was made with the setting of the sun
They were buried next to each other and lay there forever
Their tombstones are still close together
Their funeral was quiet and yet so many attended
They must have been in shock how everything had ended
The people mourned, not one tear was saved
On their tombstones two inscriptions were made
On one it reads "Their love lies here forever"
On the other it reads, "Their love was finally severed"

There's Some Good In This World… And It's Worth Fighting For

Your hand holds mine in interlaced grips
And my teeth hold on to your lower most lip
I embrace you and keep you next to me
It would almost kill me to let you go free
I want to slip off the edge of the earth and let you know
This burden is one that upon you I would never bestow
I'm sorry I hurt you like this
I wish we could have replaced it with this kiss
I never meant to hurt you
I watched as this South wind blew
I look to the South for your impending return
When I leave there is one bridge I will not burn
I've never felt this way before
There's some good left in this world and it's worth fighting for
If we give up now forever we are lost
Our fait upon the ocean will forever be tossed
I will search for you in the waking storm
Our love's breakage never will form
Should I stay and risk the pain I've dealt
At your mercy I've thankfully knelt
You drive me to the brink of insanity and leave me calm
I hope that one day you'll forget this psalm
I've found you and you've discovered me
I've realized there's no way you'll let me be
Find me faithful, find me just
I hope that one day my love you'll trust
You lost respect for me but is it coming back
Your presence is something that I wish not to lack
If you bid me away I will forever go
But remember me well when time goes by slow
We formed upon the name "Just Us"
But in all that we are where is the justice
I know I don't deserve you
But has my judgment gone askew
I write this for you, my love
Know it, and trust it well
Because it is love itself, in which I fell

To Pop The Question

There's a tree that stands alone,
A solitary forest of its own,
A ways off stands a barefaced stone,
A marriage of the two creates the peacefulness of my home

A deep-rooted quarter stairs sourly up at me,
As if it were my fault that I had let it be,
Though forgotten, it remains to be seen,
And the rust starts to form as if it were meant to bleed

Four trees and a rippled lake,
A pass of the wind, and the leaves fearfully shake,
Two beings walk below as their branches rake,
A quiet sense of trepidation passes while the silence refuses to break

You, the male, the other, the reverse,
A fumbling mind forgets what he rehearsed,
A wandering of feet that stalls this curse,
Your lips tighten, your breathing is terse

It's so quiet on these windswept days,
The country sounds a silent stage,
The starlight on these hills still wanes,
And you're too scared to ask her to stay

And it starts sometime around midnight,
The sun has gone and refuses to relight,
Your hand quivers as you gasp for respite,
A desperate grapple for the words to make things right

The curve of her body is an alluring trap that begins to beguile,
And the crickets are a melancholy soundtrack to her smile,
And that white dress she's wearing, you haven't seen it for awhile,
And her beauty waxes in the moonlight on this travelled mile

A deafening whisper that splits your world in-two,
An uncurling of the ribbons that held back a rosy hue,
And you're surprised to see her staring back at you,
A rejoicing gasp as your anxiety becomes unglued

A simple question that demands perplexity,
A perplex situation that resonates simplicity,
And I'm smiling now, as you lie next to me,
A quaint resolution of incandescent glee

www.ingramcontent.com/pod-product-compliance
Ingram Content Group UK Ltd.
Pitfield, Milton Keynes, MK11 3LW, UK
UKHW041923190726
13854UKWH00003B/1413

9 781257 912186